# Instant Chef 2

## SIMPLE MEALS FOR SMALL BUDGETS

Grant MacEwan
Community College

# Instant Chef 2

© 1994 Grant MacEwan Community College
*5th printing – January 1999*

*Compiled and edited by:*

Renate Oddy PHec, MEd

Adult Instructor

Consumer Education

**ISBN: 0-9698554-0-0**

**Canadian Cataloguing in Publication**

1. Quick and easy cookery. I.    Oddy, Renate, 1941 -     II.
Grant MacEwan Community College.
TX833.5.16  1994        641.5 55        C94-910577-5

*Printed in Canada*

# Our Thanks To

*Barb Argue and Susan Caissie:* for selecting recipes, for sharing their ideas and cooking experience, and for their dedication to this project

*Jill Murrin, Community Relations, GMCC:* for layout, design and illustrations

*Edith Villarica:* for word processing

*Patsy Price:* for her advice on publishing in Plain English

*Community Enrichment Project, Happy Cookers, Echo Valley Moms' Group, and Home Economist Betti Stretch:* for feedback, suggestions and encouragement

For further information about this publication write to:

**Consumer Education**
Grant MacEwan Community College
Mill Woods Campus
7319 – 29 Avenue
Edmonton, Alberta, Canada  T6K 2P1
**Tel.** (780) 497-4035    **Fax** (780) 497-4167

# The Story of *Instant Chef*

*W*HAT DO YOU EAT WHEN YOU ARE HUNGRY, ON A TIGHT BUDGET and don't feel like cooking? We asked residents of the House Next Door that question several years ago and compiled the first *Instant Chef* in response. Things haven't changed much since; people are still hungry and food budgets are even tighter. So we decided to put together *Instant Chef 2.* It was important to me, as an educator with the Consumer Education Project, that this cookbook would be based on the rich experience of the women I have worked with over the years. Thanks to our joint efforts you will find more recipes in this book than in the first, more practical hints and for every recipe some suggestions on how to round out the meal. We hope that the layout and design, the instructions, the language and most of all the simple ingredients will make it easy and enjoyable for you to become an "Instant Chef". &

**Renate Oddy**

# List of Recipes

*continued on next page*

# List of Recipes

# List of Recipes

# List of Recipes

# Food Shopping Tips

Everyone wants to save money when shopping for food. Check the tips to see how many things you can do to stretch your food dollar.

## Before shopping
- Look what you have on hand.
- Plan meals.
- Make a list of what you need to buy **(and take it with you!)**
- Think about buying foods that are lower in fat, sugar and sodium (salt), but high in fibre.
- Eat before you go shopping.

## At the store
- Compare prices of different sizes and brands of foods you want to buy.
- Check the bulk food section. Some bulk foods, such as spices, are a good buy.
- Read food labels carefully to find out what's inside the package.
- Use coupons only for things you usually buy.
- Buy only as much as you can use or have space to store, even if it is on special.
- Check the labels of package-mix dinners and ready-to-eat foods. These foods are easy to make but expensive. They are also usually high in fat and sodium (salt).
- Resist buying foods just because you tried a sample or saw a special display. ❧

# *E*mergency Food Shelf

| Cupboard | Fridge |
|---|---|
| • skim milk powder | • eggs |
| • pasta | • margarine |
| • rice | • cheese |
| • oats | • bread |
| • flour | • fruit |
| • soups | • vegetables (fresh, frozen) |
| • oil | • mayonnaise |
| • canned tuna, salmon | • ketchup |
| • tomato sauce | • mustard |
| • beans/lentils (canned, dry) | • soya sauce |
| • peanut butter | |
| • sugar | |
| • salt, pepper | |
| • seasonings you might find useful *(chili powder, cinnamon, italian herbs, chicken soup base)* | |
| • baking soda | |
| • potatoes | |

# Substitutions

Sometimes you may be missing an ingredient for a recipe. Can you find something else in your cupboard you can use instead?

| Use this . . . | or this . . . |
| --- | --- |
| Buttermilk  1 cup (250 mL) | 1 cup (250 mL) yogurt *or* <br> 1 cup (250 mL) milk *plus* <br> 1 tbsp (15 mL) vinegar |
| Cornstarch  1 tbsp (15 mL) | 2 tbsp (25 mL) flour |
| Dry mustard  1 tsp (5 mL) | 1 tbsp (15 mL) prepared mustard |
| One garlic clove | ⅛ tsp (0.5 mL) garlic powder |
| One small onion | 1 tbsp (15 mL) dried onion flakes |
| Fresh herbs  1 tbsp (15 mL) | 1 tsp (5 mL) dried herbs |
| Lemon juice  2 tsp (10 mL) | 1 tsp (5 mL) vinegar |
| Baking powder  1 tsp (5 mL) | ¼ tsp (1 mL) baking soda *plus* <br> ¾ tsp (3 mL) cream of tartar |
| Milk  1 cup (250 mL) | ⅓ cup (75 mL) milk powder *plus* <br> 1 cup (250 mL) water *or* <br> ½ cup (125 mL) evaporated milk *plus* <br> ½ cup (125 mL) water |

# Food Storage Tips

- Start to build an emergency shelf of basic foods so you can prepare a simple meal even when you can't go shopping.

- You don't have to buy everything at once. Divide up your list over several weeks.

- Buy only the foods that you use and have space for.

- Store dry foods in tightly sealed jars or plastic containers. Keep these in a clean, dry and cool place. Save containers from margarine, cottage cheese or ice cream for storing foods.

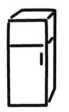

- Take your groceries home right after shopping and immediately refrigerate or freeze foods that need to stay cold.

- It is usually safe to keep meat in the refrigerator for up to 3 days. If you want to keep meat for more than 3 days, it is better to freeze it the same day you buy it. 🐌

# Food Safety Tips

### Keep food clean

- Wash hands with soap and water before handling food.
- Wash hands, cutting boards, and utensils with very hot, soapy water after handling foods, especially raw meat or chicken.

### Cook food well

- Cook meat, poultry and seafood thoroughly.
- When you reheat food be sure it is heated all the way through.

### Store food safely

- It is best to defrost meat in the fridge. This takes longer, but it is safer.
- When meat has thawed out, use it right away. Do not refreeze it.
- Cover leftovers and refrigerate them as soon as possible, even if they are still warm.
- Keep hot foods hot and cold foods cold.

### If in doubt . . . throw it out

- Throw out any food that may be unsafe.
- Be careful — you can't always smell if a food is bad. ❧

Health Canada Santé Canada

### CANADA'S
# Food Guide
## TO HEALTHY EATING

Enjoy a variety
of foods from each
group every day.

Choose lower-
fat foods
more often.

**Grain Products**
Choose whole grain
and enriched
products more
often.

**Vegetables & Fruit**
Choose dark green and
orange vegetables and
orange fruit more often.

**Milk Products**
Choose lower-fat
milk products more
often.

**Meat & Alternatives**
Choose leaner meats,
poultry and fish, as well
as dried peas, beans and
lentils more often.

Canadä

## Different People Need Different Amounts of Food

The amount of food you need every day from the 4 food groups and other foods depends on your age, body size, activity level, whether you are male or female and if you are pregnant or breast-feeding. That's why the Food Guide gives a lower and higher number of servings for each food group. For example, young children can choose the lower number of servings, while male teenagers can go to the higher number. Most other people can choose servings somewhere in between.

### Grain Products
**5-12**
SERVINGS PER DAY

**1 Serving**

Cold Cereal
1 Slice
30 g

Hot Cereal
175 mL
3/4 cup

**2 Servings**

1 Bagel, Pita or Bun

Pasta or Rice
250 mL
1 cup

### Vegetables & Fruit
**5-10**
SERVINGS PER DAY

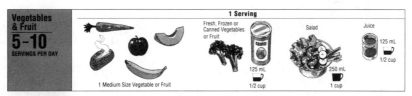

**1 Serving**

1 Medium Size Vegetable or Fruit

Fresh, Frozen or Canned Vegetables or Fruit
125 mL
1/2 cup

Salad
250 mL
1 cup

Juice
125 mL
1/2 cup

### Milk Products
SERVINGS PER DAY
Children 4–9 years: 2–3
Youth 10–16 years: 3–4
Adults: 2–4
Pregnant & Breast-feeding Women: 3–4

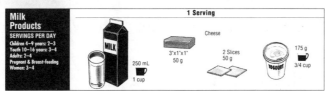

**1 Serving**

MILK
250 mL
1 cup

Cheese
3"x1"x1"
50 g

2 Slices
50 g

175 g
3/4 cup

### Other Foods

Taste and enjoyment can also come from other foods and beverages that are not part of the 4 food groups. Some of these foods are higher in fat or Calories, so use these foods in moderation.

### Meat & Alternatives
**2-3**
SERVINGS PER DAY

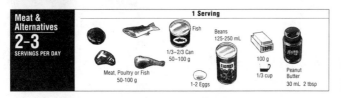

**1 Serving**

Meat, Poultry or Fish
50-100 g

Fish
1/3–2/3 Can
50–100 g

1-2 Eggs

Beans
125-250 mL

TOFU
100 g
1/3 cup

Peanut Butter
30 mL  2 tbsp

*Enjoy eating well, being active and feeling good about yourself. That's VITALIT*

© Minister of Supply and Services Canada 1992  Cat. No. H39-252/1992E  No changes permitted. Reprint permission not required.
ISBN 0-662-19648-1

*Instant Chef 2*  **xiii**

# Canada's Guidelines for Healthy Eating

- Enjoy a variety of foods.

- Emphasize cereals, breads, other grain products, vegetables and fruit.

- Choose lower fat dairy products, lean meats and foods prepared with little or no fat.

- Achieve and maintain a healthy body weight by enjoying regular physical activity and healthy eating.

- Limit salt, alcohol and caffeine. &

*For more information about healthy eating contact your local dietician or home economist.*

# Menu Planning Tips

*Canada's Food Guide to Healthy Eating* is designed to help you look good, feel great and perform at your best. "Healthy eating" means making healthy food choices over time, not just at one meal. So, plan your meals for several days or a whole week to be sure you develop a healthy pattern and get all the nutrients and energy you need. Use your menu plan as a guide, but be flexible.

## Menu planning
- helps you meet your nutritional needs
- provides the basis for your shopping list
- saves time and money
- adds interest to meals through different flavours, colours and textures of food
- helps avoid waste ❧

# What's on the menu?

| Meals | Brenda's | Tom's | Janet's | Yours |
|---|---|---|---|---|
| Breakfast | cooked cereal<br>milk<br>apple | toast with<br>peanut butter<br>& applesauce<br>milk | bran muffin<br>yogurt<br>juice<br>coffee | |
| Lunch | tuna melts<br>(p. 53)<br>cucumber<br>carrot sticks | grilled cheese<br>sandwich<br>tomato juice<br>orange | cabbage soup<br>(p. 95)<br>egg sandwich<br>apple | |
| Supper | hamburger soup<br>(p. 91)<br>garlic bread<br>yogurt, fruit | chili over rice<br>(p. 73)<br>peas<br>coleslaw<br>fruit crisp | Carol's meatballs<br>(p. 35)<br>potatoes, mixed<br>vegetables<br>tea | |
| Snack | popcorn | banana | milk & cookie | |
| Grains<br>5-12 | 6 | 7 | 5 | |
| Veg & Fruit<br>5-10 | 5 | 6 | 7 | |
| Milk<br>2-4 | 2 | 2 | 2 | |
| Meat & Alt<br>2-3 | 2 | 2 | 2 | |

# Stove Top

*E*ATING DOESN'T HAVE TO BE BORING, even on a small budget. Feel good about using lots of pasta and rice; it's economical and healthy. Experiment with different herbs and spices, a touch of salsa here, a pinch of curry there—and enjoy! 🐦

# What else can I eat with Barb's pot roast?

potatoes

carrots *or* peas

milk

oatmeal cookie

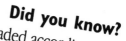

### Did you know?
- Meat is graded according to the amount of marbling or flecks of fat throughout the lean meat.

AAA — small marbling (best taste)

AA — slight marbling

A — trace marbling (less fat)

### Hint
- Barb says you can use top or bottom (outside) round or chuck roast. Chuck roast will make the sauce a little greasier.

# Barb's pot roast with dill pickles

**6 – 8 servings**
**Cooking time: 2½ – 3 hours**

| | | | | | | |
|---|---|---|---|---|---|---|
| 3 | lb | **rump roast** | 1.5 | kg | **Step 1:** | Heat oil in large sauce pan. Put roast in. Brown well on all sides. Wear oven mitts and use two large spoons when turning the roast. |
| 2 | tbsp | **oil** | 25 | mL | | |

| | | | | | | |
|---|---|---|---|---|---|---|
| 1 | large | **onion,** chopped | 1 | | **Step 2:** | Add to meat. Cover and simmer on one notch higher than low heat for about 2½ hours. Cook until meat is very tender. |
| 1 | can | **mushrooms,** drained (10 oz/284 mL) | 1 | | | |
| 10 | | **peppercorns** *or* 1 tsp (5 mL) **pepper** | 10 | | | |
| 3 | | **dill pickles,** chopped | 3 | | | |

| | | | | | | |
|---|---|---|---|---|---|---|
| 1 | cup | **light sour cream** *or* 2 tbsp/25mL **flour** | 250 | mL | **Step 3:** | Take out meat. Add flour or sour cream to liquid to make sauce. Stir till smooth. Slice meat and serve with sauce. |

## Variations

- Use ¼ cup (50 mL) water plus 1 tsp (5 mL) beef bouillon powder instead of water.
- Use ¼ cup (50 mL) dill pickle relish instead of dill pickles.
- Leave out dill pickles and sour cream for a mushroom gravy: after 2½ hours remove meat and reduce liquid by boiling a few minutes.
- Use plain yogurt instead of sour cream.

# What else can I eat with the beef and egg noodles?

cucumber salad

*or* mixed vegetables

applesauce

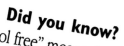

## Did you know?

- "Cholesterol free" means that the product does not contain fats from animal sources.
- A product that says "cholesterol-free" can still be high in fat. Look for nutrition information on the label.

## Hint

- Daily exercise can help you firm up your muscles, use up extra calories and lose weight.

# Beef and egg noodles

**3 – 4 servings**
**Cooking time: 20 minutes**

| | | | | | |
|---|---|---|---|---|---|
| 1 | lb | **ground beef** | 0.5 | kg | **Step 1:** In a large frying pan cook ground beef until brown. Spoon out extra fat. |
| 1 | pkg | **onion soup mix** | 1 | | **Step 2:** Stir in remaining ingredients. Heat to boiling. Reduce heat. Cover and simmer about 20 minutes until noodles are tender. Stir occasionally. |
| 1 | can | **tomatoes,** undrained (28 oz/796 mL) | 1 | | |
| 1 | can | **corn kernels,** undrained (12 oz/341 mL) | 1 | | |
| 2 | cups | **egg noodles,** uncooked | 500 | mL | |

## Variations
- Use frozen instead of canned corn.
- Add some chopped green pepper and/or celery to the beef.

# What else can I eat with the corn fritters?

tomato soup and crackers

tossed salad

milk

## Did you know?

- Pancakes can be a good choice for a simple meal. Go easy on the butter and the syrup. Top pancakes with yogurt, peanut butter and jam, and/or fruit, or mix some chopped fruit or vegetables right into the batter.

## Hint

**Try this pancake mix:**

| 2 | cups | (500 mL) | whole wheat flour |
| 3/4 | cups | (175 mL) | skim milk powder |
| 1 | tsp | (5 mL) | salt |
| 4 | tsp | (10 mL) | baking powder |
| 1/2 | cup | (125 mL) | wheat bran |

For pancakes use 1 cup mix, 1 egg and 3/4 cup water. Store remaining mix in an airtight container.

# Corn fritters

**12 fritters**
**Cooking time: 10 minutes**

| | | | | | |
|---|---|---|---|---|---|
| ½ | cup | **flour** | 125 | mL | **Step 1:** Put flour, baking powder, salt and pepper into mixing bowl. Beat in milk and egg. |
| ½ | tsp | **baking powder** | 2 | mL | |
| | | **Salt & pepper** | | | |
| ½ | cup | **milk** | 125 | mL | |
| 1 | | **egg** | 1 | | |

| | | | | | |
|---|---|---|---|---|---|
| 2 | | **cheese slices,** cut up | 2 | | **Step 2:** Stir in corn and cheese. Drop by large spoonfuls into hot oil in frying pan. Fry until crisp and golden brown. Drain on paper towel. |
| 1 | can | **corn,** drained (12 oz/341 mL) | 1 | | |
| ¼ | cup | **oil** | 50 | mL | |

## Variations

- Use grated cheddar cheese instead of cheese slices.
- Use chopped celery instead of corn.
- Use pancake mix to make thick batter. Add corn, cheese, zucchini or celery.
- Mix together a can of creamed corn, 2 tbsp (25 mL) flour, ½ tsp (2 mL) baking powder and 2 eggs, and fry.
- Use apple or banana instead of corn.

# What else can I eat with the curry in a hurry?

rice *or* noodles

broccoli, zucchini *or* salad

fresh *or* canned fruit

ice cream

## Did you know?

- Buying in bulk is not always cheaper. Be a detective and compare prices carefully.
- Whole wheat flour goes stale quickly. Only buy what you need. Store in a cool place.

## Hint

- Buy seasonings such as curry powder or pepper in the bulk section of the supermarket. You can buy just a little bit and usually save a lot of money.

# Curry in a hurry

**3–4 servings**
**Cooking time: 15 minutes**

| | | | | | |
|---|---|---|---|---|---|
| 1 | lb | **ground beef** | 0.5 | kg | **Step 1:** In large frying pan cook ground beef with onion until beef is browned. Spoon out extra fat. Sprinkle with salt and pepper. |
| 1 | small | **onion,** chopped | 1 | | |
| | | **Salt & pepper** | | | |
| ¼ | cup | **flour** | 50 | mL | **Step 2:** Mix in flour. Add milk and stir until the mixture thickens. Season with curry powder. |
| 2 | cups | **milk** | 500 | mL | |
| 1 | tsp | **curry powder** | 5 | mL | |

## Variations

• Use more curry powder.
• Add a cup of cooked peas and/or corn to the meat mixture.
• Use leftover cooked chicken or pork. Brown onion in 1 tsp (5 mL) oil. Add cooked meat and then make sauce.

# What else can I eat with Debbie's curried tuna casserole?

tossed salad *or* mixed vegetables

yogurt

muffin

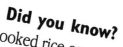

### Did you know?

• ½ cup of cooked rice or pasta equals one serving in the Grain Products group.

### Hint

• To prevent pasta from sticking together, cook it in a lot of water. Stir pasta during cooking. Rinse pasta in cold water only if you want to use it for salads or to make lasagna.

• You do not need to put oil in the water. The sauce will stick better to plain pasta.

# Debbie's curried tuna casserole

**2 – 4 servings**
**Cooking time: 30 minutes**

| | | | | |
|---|---|---|---|---|
| ½ | bag | **egg noodles** (375 g bag) | 190 | g |
| 8 | cups | **water** | 2 | L |

**Step 1:** Bring water to boil in a large pot. Add noodles. Cook till tender. Drain water off.

| | | | | |
|---|---|---|---|---|
| 1 | can | **mushroom soup** (10 oz/284 mL) | 1 | |
| ½ | cup | **milk** | 125 | mL |
| 1 | can | **tuna,** drained | 1 | |
| 1 | tsp | **curry** (or more) | 5 | mL |

**Step 2:** Stir soup, milk, tuna and curry into noodles. Heat and serve.

## Variation

• You can use 2 cups (500 mL) of cooked rice instead of the noodles.

# What else can I eat with the easy Spanish chicken & rice?

tossed salad

ice cream

## Did you know?

- Regular rice is more nutritious than instant rice. It costs a lot less than instant, and it only takes 20 minutes to cook: Bring 2 cups water to a boil. Add 1 cup rice. Reduce heat to low. Cover pot and don't peek for 20 minutes. Stir and serve.
- Add your own seasoning to rice and save even more.

## Hint

- You can take the skin off the chicken to reduce the fat.
- Put salad dressing in a squeeze bottle to reduce the amount of dressing you use.

# Easy Spanish chicken & rice

**4–8 servings**
**Cooking time: 45 minutes**

| | | | | | | |
|---|---|---|---|---|---|---|
| 1 | tbsp | **oil** | 15 | mL | | **Step 1:** Heat oil in an electric frying pan or deep skillet. Remove skin from chicken parts. Sprinkle a little salt & pepper on chicken. Brown chicken on both sides. |
| 8 | | **chicken legs,** halved *or* 6–8 **chicken parts** | 8 | | | |
| | | **Salt & pepper** | | | | |
| 2 | small | **onions,** chopped | 2 | | | **Step 2:** Add onion, garlic & seasonings. Cook for 3 minutes. |
| 4 | | **garlic cloves,** chopped | 4 | | | |
| 1 | tbsp | **paprika** | 15 | mL | | |
| | pinch | **cayenne pepper** | | pinch | | |
| ½ | tsp | **salt & pepper** | 2 | mL | | |
| 1 | can | **tomatoes,** undrained (19 oz/540 mL) | 1 | | | **Step 3:** Chop tomatoes in can. Pour tomatoes & juice into pan and stir. |
| 3 | cups | **chicken stock** *or* 3 cups **water** & 3 tsp **chicken soup base** | 750 | mL | | **Step 4:** Add stock & rice to pan. Stir. Cover and reduce heat. Simmer about 30 minutes. |
| 2 | cups | **uncooked rice** | 500 | mL | | |
| 1 | cup | **peas** (optional) | 250 | mL | | **Step 5:** Stir in peas, cover and cook for 10 more minutes. |

# *W*hat else can I eat with the fried rice?

tossed salad

milk

cookie

## Did you know?

• Cooked rice keeps well for one week. Cook more than you need and refrigerate in a covered dish. Use in fried rice recipe, or add to soups and casseroles.

## Hint

• Replace cooking water with tomato juice or broth or add soup base or a little curry for a change of flavour.

# Fried rice

**4 – 6 servings**
**Cooking time: 10 minutes**

| | | | | | |
|---|---|---|---|---|---|
| 1 | tbsp | **oil** | 15 | mL | **Step 1:** In large frying pan cook onion in oil for 2 minutes. |
| 1 | small | **onion** | 1 | | |
| 3 | cups | **rice,** cooked | 750 | mL | **Step 2:** Add rice. Cook and stir over low heat for 2 to 3 minutes. |
| ½ | cup | **ham, chicken, pork** *or* **beef,** cooked | 125 | mL | **Step 3:** Add all remaining ingredients and stir until the egg is cooked and all is heated through. |
| 1 | | **egg** | 1 | | |
| 1 | tbsp | **soy sauce** | 15 | mL | |
| | | **Salt & pepper** | | | |

## Variations

- Add cubed tofu instead of meat.
- For a one-dish meal add celery, mushrooms, peas, leftover cooked vegetables.

# What else can I eat with the hot dog skillet?

whole wheat bread

fresh *or* canned fruit

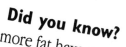

## Did you know?

- Foods with more fat have more calories.

  1 gram fat = 9 calories

  1 gram starch = 4 calories

  1 apple = 80 calories

  1 slice apple pie = 405 calories

## Hint

- Hot dogs contain a lot of fat, so choose low fat meals for the rest of the day.
- You may also want to look for lower fat turkey or chicken hot dogs.

# Hot dog skillet

**3–4 servings**
**Cooking time: 10 minutes**

| | | | | | |
|---|---|---|---|---|---|
| 1 | small | **onion,** chopped | 1 | | **Step 1:** In large frying pan cook onion in oil till tender. |
| 1 | tbsp | **oil** | 15 | mL | |

| | | | | | |
|---|---|---|---|---|---|
| 2 | cups | **corn** | 500 | mL | **Step 2:** Add all ingredients. Mix well. Cover and simmer for 5 minutes. |
| ½ | cup | **water** | 125 | mL | |
| 8 | | **wieners,** cut up | 8 | | |
| 1 | tsp | **chili powder** | 5 | mL | |
| ½ | tsp | **salt** | 2 | mL | |

| | | | | | |
|---|---|---|---|---|---|
| ¼ | cup | **Cheddar cheese,** grated | 50 | mL | **Step 3:** Sprinkle with cheese and serve. |

## Variations

- Add some green pepper when you fry the onion.
- Use frankfurters or some other sausage of your choice.
- Use light Chedder cheese.
- Instead of corn put one can of undrained sauerkraut in the frying pan. Lay cut-up wieners on top. Cover and cook for about 30 minutes.

# What else can I eat with the macaroni and cheese?

tossed salad

orange

## Did you know?

- You can make a **white sauce mix.** Store it for up to 2 months in the fridge.

2 cups (500 mL) skim milk powder
1 cup (250 mL) flour
1 cup (250 mL) soft margarine

Mix together until mixture is in fine crumbs. Cover tightly and store in refrigerator for up to 2 months.

For **1 cup sauce** combine ½ cup (125 mL) white sauce mix with 1 cup (250 mL) water in a small saucepan. Cook and stir for 2—5 minutes. Season with herbs, spices, curry and use for chicken, fish, cream soups, scalloped potatoes.

## Hint

- Add peas to whatever you can. They are a good source of fibre and quite inexpensive.
- Try this easy dessert:
Prepare a package of jello, add a can of drained fruit cocktail or peaches and refrigerate until set.

# Macaroni and cheese

2 – 3 servings
Cooking time: 20 minutes

| 1 box | **macaroni and cheese dinner** | **Step 1:** Cook according to package directions. |

## Variations

1. Slice 2 or 3 wieners, heat and add.
2. Add 1 cup (250 mL) of cooked, heated kidney beans and a little chili powder or oregano. Sprinkle with Parmesan.
3. Brown ¼ lb (125 g) ground meat with some onion and celery, drain and add.
4. Stir in ½ cup (125 mL) of drained tomatoes or 1 can tomato soup.
5. Use ¼ cup tomato sauce instead of milk.
6. Steam 1 cup (250 mL) of broccoli or cauliflower and toss with macaroni.
7. Mix in strips of cooked ham.
8. Add 1 cup (250 mL) peas or leftover cooked vegetables.
9. Add ¼ cup (50 mL) yogurt and 1 can tuna.
10. Stir into hot macaroni ½ cup (125 mL) of cottage cheese or cubed processed cheese or a little grated. Cheddar or mozzarella cheese.
11. Serve with leftover spaghetti meat sauce.
12. Add beef and tomato (#3 and 4) and bake for 10 minutes if you like.
13. Add tuna and tomato (#9 and 4), top with Parmesan and bake for 20 minutes.
14. Make your own macaroni and cheese dinner:
    Cook 1½ cups (375 mL) macaroni. Combine cooked macaroni with:

| 1½ cups (375 mL) white sauce (p. 20) | ½ tsp (2 mL) dry mustard |
| 1 tsp (5 mL) worcestershire sauce | 1 cup (250 mL) grated cheese |

# What else can I eat with the omelette?

coleslaw (p. 103)

*or* tomato slices

*or* carrot sticks

whole wheat bread

fruit yogurt

### Did you know?

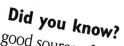

- Eggs are a good source of protein at a low price.
- One egg equals one serving of Meat and Alternatives.
- Brown shelled eggs have the same nutritional value as white ones.

### Hint

- Get together with some friends and cook enough meals for several days. Have fun and save money.

# Omelette

**1 serving**
**Cooking time: 5 minutes**

| | | | | | |
|---|---|---|---|---|---|
| 1 | tsp | **margarine** | 5 | mL | **Step 1:** Put margarine in a frying pan over medium heat. |
| 2 | | **eggs** | 2 | | **Step 2:** Break eggs into a small bowl and beat together with water, salt and pepper. |
| 1 | tbsp | **water** | 15 | mL | |
| | | **Salt & pepper** | | | |
| | | | | | **Step 3:** Turn heat to low. Pour egg mixture into pan and cook slowly. While cooking lift the edge of the omelette with a spatula and tilt the pan so the uncooked part can flow underneath. When the top is cooked, fold in half and slide onto a plate. |

## Variations

- You can use 1 whole egg and 2 egg whites in place of the 2 eggs to reduce the cholesterol.
- Place a filling (chopped ham, cheese, green onions, mushrooms) down the centre of the omelette just before you fold it over.

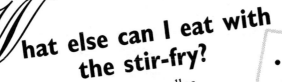

# What else can I eat with the stir-fry?

rice *or* noodles

orange whip (p. 36)

## Did you know?

• You can marinate beef. It will make it more tender and add flavour. Try this **marinade:**

| | | |
|---|---|---|
| 2 tbsp | (25 mL) | soy sauce |
| 1 tsp | (5 mL) | sugar |
| 2 tbsp | (25 mL) | cider vinegar or lemon juice |
| 2 tbsp | (25 mL) | water |

Mix and pour over meat in a plastic bag. Place bag in a bowl in the fridge for up to 24 hours. Turn meat occasionally.

## Hint

• A stir-fry is a budget stretcher — a little meat will go a long way.
• Freeze beef partially. It will be easier to slice thinly. Cut across the grain.
• You can grate ginger and freeze what you don't need.

# Stir-fry

**4 servings**
**Cooking time: 5 – 10 minutes**

| | | | | | |
|---|---|---|---|---|---|
| ½ | lb | **beef, pork** *or* **chicken** | 250 | g | **Step 1:** Cut meat into very thin strips. |
| 2 | tbsp | **oil** | 25 | mL | **Step 2:** In a large pan heat oil till very hot. Add meat. Stir-fry for 2 minutes or until meat is done. Take out of pan. |
| 1 | small | **onion,** sliced | 1 | | **Step 3:** Stir-fry onion, garlic, ginger and carrots for one minute. Add broccoli and stir-fry for 2 minutes. Return meat to pan. |
| 1 | | **garlic clove,** chopped | 1 | | |
| 1 | tsp | **ginger** | 5 | mL | |
| 1 | cup | **carrots,** sliced | 250 | mL | |
| 2 | cups | **broccoli pieces** | 500 | mL | |
| ⅓ | cup | **water** | 75 | mL | **Step 4:** Mix ingredients for the sauce. Pour over meat and vegetables and cook till thickened. |
| 2 | tbsp | **soy sauce** | 25 | mL | |
| 1 | tbsp | **cornstarch** | 15 | mL | |

## Variations

- Use leftover meat, chicken, turkey.
- Use any vegetables of your choice: celery, mushrooms, cabbage, bean sprouts, green onion, zucchini, green pepper.
- Make a tofu stir-fry. Marinate tofu ahead of time. Add a little cornstarch to the marinade and use it to make the sauce.

# Oven Baked

AKE THE MOST OF YOUR OVEN and cook a whole meal at once. Better still, cook a double batch and freeze a portion of it. You'll save time and energy that way. You may have to wait a little longer before you can eat, but the aroma of something cooking in the oven will tempt your appetite. Eat—and enjoy! ⤳

## Recipes in this section

# What else can I eat with Barb's chicken pizzarella?

noodles

steamed carrots

*and/or* zucchini

fresh fruit

## Did you know?

- Less fat in your diet is better for your heart and your weight.
- Remove the skin from the chicken pieces. Use part skim mozzarella cheese to reduce the fat of this meal.

## Hint

- Compare the fat in this recipe (chicken only):

  skin removed     3 tsp fat/serving (= 13 g)

  skin included     9 tsp fat/serving (= 38 g)

# Barb's chicken pizzarella

**4 – 6 servings**
**350°F/180°C**
**Cooking time: 45 minutes**

| | | | | | |
|---|---|---|---|---|---|
| | | | | | **Step 1:** Turn oven on. |
| 2 | lbs | **chicken parts,** skinned (6 – 8 pieces) | 1 | kg | **Step 2:** Put chicken pieces into a 9" x 13" (3.5 L) pan. |
| 1 | can | **tomato sauce** (7½ oz / 213 mL) | 1 | | **Step 3:** Combine ingredients and pour sauce over chicken. Bake uncovered for 45 minutes. |
| 1 | can | **mushrooms,** drained (10 oz / 284 mL) | 1 | | |
| 1 | tbsp | **onion flakes,** dried | 15 | mL | |
| ½ | tsp | **oregano** | 2 | mL | |
| 1 | | **garlic clove,** chopped | 1 | | |
| 1 | cup | **part skim mozzarella cheese,** shredded | 250 | mL | **Step 4:** Sprinkle cheese over chicken. Return to oven for 5 minutes until cheese melts. |

**Variation**

• Use 1 can of spaghetti sauce instead of tomato sauce.

# *W*hat else can I eat with the canny casserole?

baked potato *or* pasta
carrot salad

## Did you know?

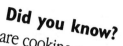

- When you are cooking a casserole or meat loaf in the oven, save time and money by cooking vegetables and dessert in the oven too.
- You can turn the oven off a few minutes before total baking time is up.

## Hint

- Bake a few extra potatoes for another meal: Slice leftover potatoes ¼"–½" (.5–1.5 cm) thick, season with salt and pepper and fry, or brush with oil and broil.

# Canny casserole

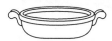

**3 servings**
**350°F/180°C**
**Cooking time: 1 hour**

**Step 1:** Turn oven on. Grease casserole dish.

| | | | |
|---|---|---|---|
| 2 | | **eggs** | 2 |
| ½ | cup | **evaporated milk** | 125 mL |
| 1 | can | **cream style corn**<br>(14 oz/398 mL) | 1 |
| 1 | can | **tuna** | 1 |
| 1 | small | **green pepper,** chopped | 1 |
| 1 | small | **onion,** finely chopped | 1 |

**Step 2:** Mix all ingredients together. Pour into casserole and bake uncovered for 1 hour.

## Variation

Use ½ cup (125 mL) chopped celery instead of green pepper.

# What else can I eat with Carol's meatballs?

potatoes *or* noodles

peas *or* carrots *or* corn

ice cream

## Did you know?

- Foods like potatoes, bread, or pasta are not fattening. It is what you add to them that makes them high in calories.

1 baked potato = 100 calories

1 baked potato plus 1 tbsp butter or margarine = 200 calories

## Hint

- You can cook the meatballs in an electric frying pan if you like.

# Carol's meatballs

**20 – 24 balls**
**350°F / 180°C**
**Cooking time: 45 – 60 minutes**

**Step 1:** Turn oven on.

| | | | | | |
|---|---|---|---|---|---|
| 1 | lb | **ground beef,** lean | 0.5 | kg | |
| 1 | | **egg** | 1 | | |
| 1 | pkg | **onion soup mix** | 1 | | |
| 1 | cup | **rice,** raw | 250 | mL | |

**Step 2:** Mix hamburger with the other ingredients and form 20–24 balls and place in 2 qt (2 L) casserole dish.

| | | | | |
|---|---|---|---|---|
| 1 | can | **tomato soup** (10 oz / 284 mL) | 1 | |
| 1 | can | **water** | 1 | |

**Step 3:** Mix soup and water. Pour over meatballs and cook for about 45 minutes

## Variation

*Sweet and Sour Meatballs*

Instead of tomato soup pour this sauce over the meatballs:

| | | | | |
|---|---|---|---|---|
| ⅓ | cup | **brown sugar** | 75 | mL |
| 1 | tbsp | **cornstarch** | 15 | mL |
| 1 | cup | **pineapple tidbits & juice** | 250 | mL |
| 2 | tbsp | **vinegar** | 25 | mL |
| 1 | tbsp | **soya sauce** | 15 | mL |
| 1 | small | **green pepper,** chopped | 1 | |

# *W*hat else can I eat with the cheesy hashbrowns?

bean salad (p. 107)
*or* Caesar salad with tuna
fruit crisp (p. 115)

### Did you know?
- Packages of grated cheese are sometimes cheaper than block cheese. Check the unit price (price per 100 g).
- For 1 cup grated cheese you need ¼ lb (125 g) block cheese.

### Hint
- You can double or triple this recipe.
- **Orange whip** is a light dessert. Beat together till peaks form:

| | | |
|---|---|---|
| ½ cup | (125 mL) | ice cold water |
| 2 tbsp | (25 mL) | lemon juice |
| ⅔ cup | (175 mL) | skim milk powder |

Beat in:

| | | |
|---|---|---|
| ⅓ cup | (75 mL) | sugar |
| 3 tbsp | (50 mL) | orange juice concentrate |

# Cheesy hashbrowns

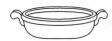

**4 servings**
**350°F/180°C**
**Cooking time: 30–40 minutes**

**Step 1:** Turn oven on. Grease 9" x 13" (3.5 L) baking dish.

| | | | | |
|---|---|---|---|---|
| 4 | cups | **hashbrowns,** frozen | 1 | L |
| 1 | cup | **cheddar cheese,** grated | 250 | mL |
| 1 | cup | **light sour cream** | 250 | mL |
| 3 | | **green onions,** chopped | 3 | |
| 1 | can | **mushroom soup** (10 oz/284 mL) | 1 | |
| ½ | cup | **milk** | 125 | mL |

**Step 2:** Mix all ingredients together and put into baking dish.
Bake uncovered for 30–40 minutes.

## Variations

- Use yogurt instead of sour cream.
- Use celery soup or cream of chicken soup instead of mushroom soup.
- Grate leftover cooked potatoes and use instead of hashbrowns.
- Add leftover fried crumbled bacon.
- You can double or triple this recipe

# What else can I eat with the fast pizza-style fish?

toasted garlic bread

tossed salad

ice cream

## Did you know?

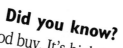

- Fish is a good buy. It's high in protein, low in fat and a source of vitamins and minerals.
- Breaded and fried fish is convenient, but it is expensive and very high in fat.

## Hint

- Allow 10 minutes cooking time per inch (2.5 cm) thickness for fresh fish, 20 minutes per inch for frozen fish. The cooking time is the same for all cooking methods.

# Fast pizza-style fish

**4 servings**
**450°F/230°C**
**Cooking time: 10 minutes**

**Step 1:** Turn oven on.
Grease 7" x 11" (2 L) pan.

| | | | | |
|---|---|---|---|---|
| 1 | lb | **fish fillets** of your choice | 0.5 | kg |

**Step 2:** Place fillets in greased baking dish.

| | | | | |
|---|---|---|---|---|
| ½ | cup | **tomato sauce** | 125 | mL |
| ¼ | cup | **green pepper,** chopped | 50 | mL |
| ¼ | cup | **parsley,** chopped | 50 | mL |
| ½ | tsp | **basil,** dried | 2 | mL |
| 1 | cup | **part-skim mozzarella cheese,** shredded | 250 | mL |

**Step 3:** Spoon tomato sauce on top. Sprinkle with green pepper, seasonings and cheese.
Bake for 10 minutes or until bubbly and fish flakes easily when you test it with a fork.

## Variation

• You can use frozen fish fillets. Thaw slightly before baking and cook a little longer.

# What else can I eat with the impossible cheeseburger pie?

potatoes
glazed carrots
cucumber salad
orange whip (p. 36)

### Did you know?

- You can make your own biscuit mix:

| | | |
|---|---|---|
| 4 cups | (1 L) | flour |
| 1 cup | (250 mL) | milk powder |
| 7 tsp | (35 mL) | baking powder |
| 1 tsp | (5 mL) | salt |
| ¾ cup | (175 mL) | shortening |

Mix and store covered in a cool place.

### Hint

- You don't have to make a crust for this pie. The crust forms by itself as it bakes.
- You can use the biscuit mix for pancakes, scones or dumplings.

# Impossible cheeseburger pie

**4 – 6 servings**
**400°F / 200°C**
**Cooking time: 25 – 30 minutes**

**Step 1:** Turn oven on. Grease deep 10" (25 cm) pie plate or baking dish.

| | | | | |
|---|---|---|---|---|
| 1 | lb | **ground beef** | 0.5 | kg |
| 2 | med | **onions** | 2 | |
| | | **Salt & pepper** | | |

**Step 2:** Cook beef and onion until beef is brown. Spoon out extra fat. Season with salt and pepper. Spread beef in greased pie plate.

| | | | | |
|---|---|---|---|---|
| 1 | cup | **biscuit mix** | 250 | mL |
| 1½ | cups | **milk** | 375 | mL |
| 3 | | **eggs** | 3 | |

**Step 3:** Beat all together and pour over beef in pie plate. Bake for 25 minutes.

| | | | | |
|---|---|---|---|---|
| 2 | | **tomatoes**, sliced | 2 | |
| ½ | cup | **cheese**, grated | 125 | mL |

**Step 4:** Top with tomato slices and cheese and bake for another 5–10 minutes. The pie is done if you insert a knife and it comes out clean.

## Variations

- Impossible Tuna Pie: Fry 2 chopped onions. Mix in 2 cans of tuna. Pour into pie plate. Then do steps 3 and 4.
- Impossible Broccoli Pie: Spread uncooked, chopped broccoli and some finely chopped onion into pie plate. Then do steps 3 and 4.
- Mixed Vegetable Pie: Sauté onion, green pepper, corn, mushroom, zucchini. Then do steps 3 and 4.

# *W*hat else can I eat with the layered supper casserole?

coleslaw (p. 103)
milk

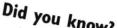

## Did you know?
* One serving of meat and alternatives equals:
  2–4 oz (50–100 g) meat, poultry or fish,
  1–2 eggs, or
  ½–1 cup (125–250 mL) baked beans

## Hint
* Pasta is in! Try using whole wheat macaroni or spaghetti for extra nutrition, or different shapes for interest.

# Layered supper casserole

**3 – 4 servings**
**350°F/180°C**
**Cooking time: 30 minutes**

|  |  |  |  |  |
|---|---|---|---|---|
|  |  |  |  | **Step 1:** Turn oven on. Grease a 2 qt (2 L) casserole dish. |
| 1 | cup | **macaroni** | 250 mL | **Step 2:** Cook macaroni in boiling water. |
| 4 | cups | **water** | 1 L | Drain well. |
| ½ | lb | **ground beef** | 250 g | **Step 3:** Combine ground beef, onion and |
| 1 | small | **onion,** chopped | 1 | cook until brown. Spoon out extra fat. |
| 1 | cup | **corn,** canned or frozen | 250 mL | Add corn and seasoning. Put layers of |
|  |  | **Salt & pepper** |  | beef and macaroni in a greased dish. |
| 1 | can | **tomato soup** (10 oz/284 mL) | 1 | **Step 4:** Put soup and cheese on top. |
| ½ | cup | **cheese,** grated | 125 mL | Bake for 30 min. |

## Variations

• Use spaghetti instead of macaroni.

• Add some peas.

## What else can I eat with the saucy hamburger?

rice *or* noodles *or* mashed potatoes

milk pudding

*or* fresh fruit in yogurt

### Did you know?

Maximum fat (by raw weight)
**Ground beef:**

| | |
|---|---|
| regular | 30% |
| medium | 23% |
| lean | 17% |
| extra lean | 10% |

### Hint

- Regular ground beef is usually the best buy. Use it when you can pour off the fat.
- You may also rinse the cooked ground beef with hot water.

# Saucy hamburger

**3 – 4 servings**
**350°F/180°C**
**Cooking time: 20 minutes**

|  |  |  |  |  |  |
|---|---|---|---|---|---|
|  |  |  |  |  | **Step 1:** Turn oven on. |
| 2 | cups | **mixed vegetables** | 500 | mL | **Step 2:** Cook vegetables in boiling water for |
| 1 | cup | **water** | 250 | mL | 5 minutes. Drain. |
| 1 | lb | **ground beef** | 0.5 | kg | **Step 3:** Brown ground beef in frying pan. Spoon out extra fat. |
| 1 | tbsp | **flour** | 25 | mL | **Step 4:** Stir flour into beef. |
| 1 | can | **tomato sauce** (7½ oz/213 mL) | 1 |  | **Step 5:** Add vegetables, sauce, tomatoes, water and salt. Pour into large casserole. Bake uncovered for 20 minutes. |
| 1 | can | **tomatoes** (14 oz/398 mL) |  |  |  |
| ¼ | cup | **water** | 50 | mL |  |
| ½ | tsp | **salt** | 2 | mL |  |

## Variations

- Fry a chopped onion with the meat.
- Use crushed tomatoes instead of whole tomatoes.
- If you use an electric frying pan, finish cooking the meal in the frying pan instead of the oven.
- You can add uncooked vegetables, but baking time will be 20 minutes longer.

# What else can I eat with the souped-up meatloaf?

potatoes

green beans *or* peas

coleslaw (p. 103)

*or* fruit crisp (p. 115)

*or* fresh fruit

## Did you know?

- The fat in food gives you a lot of calories and very few nutrients.
- Many foods have more fat than you think:
Regular bologna (2 oz) or a hot dog have 4 tsp of fat.
Turkey bologna (2 oz) has 2 tsp of fat.

## Hint

- Save an empty can for draining fat into. When the fat is solid you can throw the can away.

# Souped-up meatloaf

**4 servings**
**350°F / 180°C**
**Cooking time: 45 minutes**

**Step 1:** Turn oven on.

| | | | | | |
|---|---|---|---|---|---|
| 1 | lb | **ground beef** | 0.5 | kg | |
| ½ | cup | **oats** *or* **bread crumbs** | 125 | mL | |
| 1 | | **onion,** finely chopped | 1 | | |
| 1 | | **egg** | 1 | | |
| ¼ | cup | **ketchup** | 50 | mL | |
| | | **Salt & pepper** | | | |

**Step 2:** In a large bowl mix all ingredients together. Place into loaf pan and bake for 30 minutes.

| | | | | |
|---|---|---|---|---|
| 1 | can | **tomato soup** (10 oz / 284 mL) | 1 | |

**Step 3:** Use oven mitts and take out pan. Pour grease into an empty can. Pour tomato soup over the loaf and bake another 15 minutes.

## Variations

• Use mushroom soup instead of tomato soup.
• Put cheese slices on top for last few minutes of baking.
• Use 2 tbsp/25 mL tomato paste instead of ketchup. This makes the meatloaf less salty.
• For a change in flavour add other seasonings, such as garlic, Worcestershire sauce, parsley, thyme.

# *W*hat else can I eat with Susan's winning chuckwagon beans?

whole wheat bread/buns

Caesar salad

### Did you know?

- 1 cup (250 mL) of baked beans gives you half the fibre you need in a day!

### Hint

- This meal is high in sodium (sodium is a part of salt). To reduce the sodium in this meal look for low or no salt tomato sauce, add less or no salt, or use a low-sodium bouillon cube.

# Susan's winning chuckwagon beans

4 – 6 servings
375°F/190°C
Cooking time: 40 – 45 minutes

**Step 1:** Turn oven on.

| | | | | |
|---|---|---|---|---|
| 1 | lb | **ground beef** | 0.5 | kg |
| 1 | | **garlic clove,** chopped | 1 | |
| 2 | small | **onions,** chopped | 2 | |
| ½ | cup | **celery,** chopped | 125 | mL |

**Step 2:** Fry ground beef and vegetables until tender. Spoon out extra fat.

| | | | | |
|---|---|---|---|---|
| 1 | cube | **beef bouillon** | 1 | |
| ½ | cup | **water** | 125 | mL |
| 1 | tbsp | **mustard** | 15 | mL |
| 1 | can | **tomato sauce** (7½ oz/213 mL) | 1 | |
| 1 | can | **pork and beans** (28 oz/796 mL) | 1 | |
| | | **Salt & pepper** | | |

**Step 3:** Dissolve bouillon cube in water. Add to meat mixture with remaining ingredients. Bake in covered 2 qt (2 L) casserole dish for 40 – 45 minutes.

## Variations

• Use beef soup base in place of bouillon cube.

• Fry 6 slices of bacon until crisp. Drain and crumble on beans just before serving.

# What else can I eat with the toad in the hole?

peas *or* beans

sliced tomato

cookie

apple

## Did you know?

- Whole grains are a good choice. They are a good source of fibre and other nutrients.
- You can replace half of the flour in most recipes with whole wheat flour.

## Hint

- You can use the batter by itself to make yorkshire pudding or popovers.

## Toad in the hole

**4 servings**
**425°F (220°C)**
**Cooking time: 25 – 30 minutes**

| | | | | | |
|---|---|---|---|---|---|
| 1 | lb | **sausages** *or* **wieners** | 500 | g | **Step 1:** Turn oven on. Place sausages or wieners in a 1½ qt (1.5 L) baking dish and put in oven. |

| | | | | | |
|---|---|---|---|---|---|
| 3 | | **eggs** | 3 | | **Step 2:** Beat well together. |
| 2 | cups | **milk** | 500 | mL | |
| 1 | cup | **flour** | 250 | mL | |
| ½ | tsp | **salt** | 2 | mL | |

**Step 3:** Take baking dish out of oven. Spoon out extra fat. Pour batter over sausages. Return to oven. Bake till puffy and golden brown. Cut in squares and serve right away.

**Note:** The batter rises during baking but will fall when you take it out of the oven.

### Variation

• Cut sausages in half or wieners in quarters and bake in a muffin tin.

# What else can I eat with the tuna melts?

tomato wedges

carrot sticks

milk

### Did you know?
- You can prepare the tuna mixture ahead of time and bake it when you need it.
- You can add the cheese to the tuna mixture or sprinkle it on top.

### Hint
- Look for cheese with less than 20% fat.
- Use pitas or hamburger buns made with whole wheat.

# Tuna melts

**2 – 3 servings**
**375°F/190°C**
**Cooking time: 10 minutes**

**Step 1:** Turn oven on.

| | | | | |
|---|---|---|---|---|
| 1 | can | **tuna** (water packed), drained | 1 | |
| ½ | cup | **celery,** chopped | 125 | mL |
| 2 | | **green onions,** chopped | 2 | |
| ⅓ | cup | **light mayonnaise** *or* **salad dressing** | 75 | mL |
| ½ | cup | **light Cheddar** *or* **part-skim mozzarella cheese,** grated | 125 | mL |

**Step 2:** Drain tuna and mix together with the other ingredients.

| | | | |
|---|---|---|---|
| 3 | | **pitas** *or* **hamburger buns** | 3 |

**Step 3:** Place pitas or buns on cookie sheet. Spread with tuna mixture. Bake for about 10 minutes or until brown.

## Variations

• Add 1 tsp (5 mL) lemon juice and ¼ tsp (1 mL) curry powder.
• Add 2 tbsp (25 mL) pickle relish.

# Meatless

$\mathcal{P}$LANNING MEALS WITHOUT meat is not difficult. Use the Canada Food Guide to help you. Have a variety of foods and include meat alternatives such as dried beans, peas, lentils and tofu. Mix and match these with a variety of grains and/or lower fat dairy products. Experiment with "meatless Mondays"—and enjoy! ❧

# What else can I eat with the bean burritos?

light sour cream, salsa, green onion

tossed salad

milk

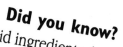

### Did you know?

• Salt and acid ingredients (eg. tomatoes) make beans tough. Add them after the beans are cooked.

• Drain and rinse cooked beans. This helps reduce the gas some people suffer from.

### Hint

• Some people like to add a little cooked ground beef, chicken or turkey to the beans, but vegetarians leave out the meat.

# Bean burritos

**10 burritos**
**Cooking time: 15 minutes**

| | | | | | |
|---|---|---|---|---|---|
| 1 | tbsp | **oil** | 15 | mL | |
| 1 | small | **onion,** chopped | 1 | | |
| 3 | | **garlic cloves,** chopped | 3 | | |
| 1 | tsp | **salt** | 5 | mL | |
| 2 | tsp | **cumin** | 10 | mL | |
| 5 | cups | **pinto beans,** cooked,* mashed | 1.25 | L | |

**Step 1:** In a frying pan fry onion, garlic and seasonings in oil for 2–3 minutes. Add beans and cook for 10 minutes stirring all the time.

| | | | | | |
|---|---|---|---|---|---|
| 10 | | **flour tortillas** | 10 | | |
| 2 | cups | **cheese,** grated | 500 | mL | |
| | | **Salsa** | | | |

**Step 2:** Spread ½ cup of refried bean mixture down the centre of a warm tortilla. Add a little cheese and salsa. Fold 2" of the tortilla up over the filling and roll up.

## Variations

- Make all 10 burritos and freeze leftovers. They make a great lunch to take along and are easy to heat up in a microwave.
- Use 2 cans (19 oz/540 mL) of pinto, romano or kidney beans.
- Place burritos in a baking dish. Cover with tomato sauce and a little cheese and bake.

*For cooking instructions, see page 106.

# What else can I eat with the cottage cheese loaf?

tomato *or* mushroom sauce
tossed salad
bran muffin (p. 114)

## Did you know?
- Low fat sour cream substitute: In blender put 1 cup 1% cottage cheese, 1 tbsp lemon juice, ¼ tsp salt. Blend till smooth. Stir in some onion or chives.
- Use as a dip for fresh vegetables or as a topping for perogies, baked potatoes, etc.

## Hint
- This loaf is good cold. Slice and put in a bun with some lettuce.
- Cottage cheese is a good source of protein and calcium. Use the low fat variety.

# Cottage cheese loaf

**3 – 4 servings**
**350°F / 180°C**
**Baking time: 40 – 45 minutes**

**Step 1:** Turn oven on. Grease a small loaf pan.

| | | | | |
|---|---|---|---|---|
| 1 | small | **onion,** chopped | 1 | |
| ½ | cup | **celery,** chopped | 125 | mL |
| 1 | small | **carrot,** grated | 1 | |
| 2 | tbsp | **oil** | 30 | mL |
| 2 | cups | **cottage cheese** | 500 | mL |
| 1 | cup | **dry bread crumbs** | 250 | mL |
| 2 | | **eggs** | 2 | |
| 1 | tsp | **salt** | 5 | mL |
| ½ | tsp | **pepper** | 2 | mL |

**Step 2:** In large bowl combine all ingredients. Place in baking dish and bake for 35–40 min.

## Variations

- Cook vegetables in oil until softened before adding to remaining ingredients.
- Use 2 cups of fresh bread crumbs instead of dry.
- Add some chopped walnuts. This gives some texture.
- Add 1 tbsp (15 mL) of lemon juice.
- Leave out the grated carrot.
- Add some soy sauce for flavor.

# What else can I eat with the lazy lasagna?

three bean salad

or carrots & celery sticks

### Did you know?

- "Legumes" are dried beans, peas and lentils. They have more protein than any other vegetable and are an alternative to meat. When they are served with a grain product such as whole grain bread, they form a complete protein.

### Hint

- 1 lb (500 g) cheese gives you 4 cups (1 L) grated cheese.

# Lazy lasagna

2 – 3 servings
375°F/190°C
Baking time: 15 – 20 minutes

| | | | | | |
|---|---|---|---|---|---|
| | | | | | **Step 1:** Turn oven on. Grease a 2 qt (2 L) baking dish. |
| 1 | lb | **perogies,** any kind | 0.5 | kg | **Step 2:** Cook perogies in boiling water for 3 minutes. Drain. |
| 1 | can | **tomato soup** (10 oz/284 mL) | 1 | | **Step 3:** Place perogies on the bottom of the baking dish in a single layer. Cover with cottage cheese. Mix oregano into soup and pour over cottage cheese layer. Sprinkle with cheese. Bake for 15–20 minutes. |
| ½ | tsp | **oregano** | 2 | mL | |
| 1 | cup | **cottage cheese,** creamed | 250 | mL | |
| 1 | cup | **part-skim mozzarella,** grated | 250 | mL | |

## Variation

• To make a perogy casserole: Sauté 1 chopped onion and 1 chopped green pepper. Mix with a package of frozen perogies, 4 chopped hard boiled eggs, a little milk and 1 can of mushroom soup. Bake for 35 minutes at 350°F/180°C.

# What else can I eat with the mock hamburgers?

bun

lettuce, tomato

oven baked fries

chocolate milk

### Did you know?

- Tofu is made from soy beans.
- Tofu is low in saturated fats and calories. Because it is made from a vegetable product, it is cholesterol free.

### Hint

- Save some thick porridge from breakfast and make mock hamburgers for the next day.
- **Oven baked fries** are easy. Cut clean potatoes into 8 wedges. Toss in plastic bag with 1 tbsp oil, a little garlic, chili powder or Parmesan cheese. Bake at 400° for 30 minutes.

# Mock hamburgers

**4 patties**
**Cooking time: 10 – 15 minutes**

| | | | | | |
|---|---|---|---|---|---|
| 1 | large | **potato,** raw and grated | 1 | | **Step 1:** In frying pan cook potato and onion in oil. |
| ½ | small | **onion,** chopped | ½ | | |
| 2 | tbsp | **oil** | 25 | mL | |

| | | | | | |
|---|---|---|---|---|---|
| 1 | cup | **oatmeal,** cooked | 250 | mL | **Step 2:** Mix remaining ingredients together. Make patties and fry in a little oil. |
| ½ | cup | **walnuts,** chopped fine | 125 | mL | |
| ¾ | cup | **bread crumbs,** dry | 175 | mL | |
| 1 | | **egg** | 1 | | |
| 1 | tbsp | **soya sauce** | 15 | mL | |
| | | **Salt** | | | |

**Variation**

• Tofu burger: Sauté 1 chopped onion. Mix with 1 lb medium-firm mashed tofu, 1 cup bread crumbs, 2 eggs, soya sauce and seasonings to taste. Form into patties and fry.

# What else can I eat with the pasta and beans?

peas
*and/or* tossed salad
chocolate pudding

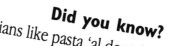

### Did you know?

- Italians like pasta 'al dente'. This means "firm to the bite".

### Hint

- Most dried pastas double in volume during cooking. Egg noodles, however, will stay the same size.
- 1 lb (500 g) uncooked macaroni gives you 4 cups (1 L) uncooked macaroni or 8 cups (2 L) cooked macaroni.

# Pasta and beans

**4 – 6 servings**
**Cooking time: 20 minutes**

| | | | | |
|---|---|---|---|---|
| 1 can | **spaghetti sauce** (28 oz / 796 mL) | 1 | **Step 1:** | In a large pot bring sauce to boil. Add beans. Turn down heat and simmer for 20 minutes. |
| 1 can | **kidney beans,** drained (19 oz / 540 mL) | 1 | | |
| 1 lb | **pasta** (shells, spirals, rigatoni) | 500 g | **Step 2:** | Cook pasta in lots of boiling water until al dente. Drain. |
| | **Parsley** (optional) **Parmesan cheese** | | **Step 3:** | Serve sauce over pasta with parsley and grated Parmesan cheese. |

## Variation

• Make your own meatless spaghetti sauce: Sauté onion and garlic in a little oil. Add a large can of tomatoes and some Italian seasoning and simmer 15 minutes.

# What else can I eat with the polenta bake?

carrots

*or* spinach au gratin

## Did you know?

- Polenta comes to us from Italy. But most recipes using corn come from Central and South America, for example, tacos, nachos, tortillas, enchiladas.

## Hint

- Try serving **spinach au gratin** with polenta: Place lightly cooked spinach in a baking dish. Pour one cup of tomato sauce over. Sprinkle with a little Parmesan. Bake for 10 minutes.

# Polenta bake

**3 – 4 servings**
**350°F / 180°C**
**Baking time: 35 – 40 minutes**

**Step 1:** Turn oven on. Grease a 2 qt (2 L) baking dish.

| | | | | |
|---|---|---|---|---|
| 2½ | cups | **milk** | 625 | mL |
| ¾ | cup | **cornmeal** | 175 | mL |

**Step 2:** In a saucepan with a heavy bottom beat cornmeal into cold milk with a wire whisk. Bring mixture to a boil, stirring all the time. Cook over low heat till thick (about 5 minutes).

| | | | | |
|---|---|---|---|---|
| 1 | cup | **light cheddar cheese,** grated | 250 | mL |
| 3 | | **eggs,** beaten | 3 | |

**Step 3:** Stir in cheese and eggs. Pour into baking dish. Bake for 35 – 40 minutes.

## Variations
- Add green onions to milk.
- Cook the cornmeal. Pour into a greased pie plate and refrigerate for one hour. Cut into wedges and serve with tomato sauce and Parmesan cheese or use a pizza crust.
- Serve leftover polenta for lunch.

# What else can I eat with the potato kugel?

rice pudding
fresh fruit

## Did you know?
- This meal has all the important nutrients built in:
  - Grain products—oats & rice
  - Vegetables & fruit—potatoes, carrots
  - Milk products—skim milk & cheese
  - Meat & alternatives—eggs

## Hint
- You can serve this dish hot or cold.
- The potatoes may turn black during grating, but the colour will not affect the taste.

# Potato kugel

**4 – 6 servings**
**350°F / 180°C**
**Baking time: 45 minutes**

**Step 1:** Turn oven on. Grease 2 qt (2 L) baking dish.

| | | | | |
|---|---|---|---|---|
| 6 | med | **potatoes** | 6 | |
| 3 | med | **carrots** | 3 | |
| 1 | small | **onion** | 1 | |

**Step 2:** Grate potatoes, carrots and onion in a large bowl.

| | | | | |
|---|---|---|---|---|
| 1 | | **garlic clove**, chopped | 1 | |
| 2 | | **eggs** | 2 | |
| 2 | tbsp | **oil** | 25 | mL |
| 2 | tsp | **salt** | 10 | mL |
| ¼ | cup | **rolled oats** | 50 | mL |
| 1 | cup | **skim milk powder** | 250 | mL |

**Step 3:** Stir in all the ingredients. Spread mixture into greased baking dish. Bake for 45 min.

| | | | | |
|---|---|---|---|---|
| 1 | cup | **light cheese**, grated | 250 | mL |

**Step 4:** Take dish out, sprinkle cheese on top. Return to oven for about 5 minutes until cheese is melted.

## Variations

- A simpler version: leave out carrots and cheese.
- Fry the onions in a little oil until soft, then add to potatoes.
- Use ½ tsp (2 mL) garlic powder instead of 1 garlic clove.

# What else can I eat with the quick chili over rice?

cabbage *or* fruit salad

milk

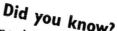

### Did you know?

• For something different, try serving the chili over *couscous*. You can find it packaged or in the bulk section of large supermarkets. Bring 1½ cups water to boil. Add 1½ cups couscous and 1 tbsp oil. Cover and remove from heat. Let stand for 5 min. Fluff with a fork and serve.

### Hint

• You don't really need meat to make chili. To get used to a meatless chili try using a little less meat each time you make chili.

• If you have time, cook brown rice. It takes about 45 minutes to cook, but it is more nutritious than the white.

# Quick chili over rice

**3 – 4 servings**
**Cooking time: 20 minutes**

| | | | | |
|---|---|---|---|---|
| 3 | cups | **water** | 750 | mL |
| 1½ | cups | **rice** | 375 | mL |

**Step 1:** In a large pot bring water to boil. Add rice and stir. Bring to boil again. Turn down heat to very low. Cover and cook for 15–20 minutes. Don't peek until time is up.

| | | | | |
|---|---|---|---|---|
| 1 | tbsp | **oil** | 15 | mL |
| ¼ | cup | **onion**, chopped | 50 | mL |
| ¼ | cup | **green pepper**, chopped | 50 | mL |
| 1 | | **garlic clove** | 1 | |

**Step 2:** Cook vegetables in oil for 5 minutes.

| | | | |
|---|---|---|---|
| 1 | can | **tomato sauce** (28 oz/796 mL) | 1 |
| 1 | can | **kidney beans,** drained (19 oz/540 mL) | 1 |
| | | **Salt & pepper** | |
| | | **Chili powder** | |

**Step 3:** Add to vegetables. Season to taste. Simmer for 10–15 minutes. Serve over rice.

## Variations

- Sprinkle each serving with a little grated cheese.
- Add a little mashed tofu to the sauce.
- Add ¼ cup (50 mL) bulgur to sauce to add some texture.

# *W*hat else can I eat with the spinach-cheese bake?

tomato slices
blueberry *or* bran muffin (p. 114)
milk

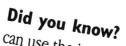

### Did you know?

- Your body can use the iron from the spinach better if you have some food that is higher in Vitamin C at the same meal.

### Hint

- Experiment with no-name brands; but be careful, they are not always cheaper.

# Spinach-cheese bake

**3 – 4 servings**
**350°F / 180°C**
**Baking time: 40 minutes**

**Step 1:** Grease baking dish.

| | | | | | |
|---|---|---|---|---|---|
| 8 | | **bread slices,** white | 8 | | |
| 2 | tbsp | **margarine** | 25 | mL | |

**Step 2:** Spread margarine thinly on both sides of bread. Lay 4 slices on bottom of baking dish.

| | | | | | |
|---|---|---|---|---|---|
| 1 | pkg | **spinach,** cooked (10 oz / 280 g) | 1 | | |
| ¼ | cup | **onion,** finely chopped | 50 | mL | |
| 1 | cup | **light Cheddar cheese,** grated | 250 | mL | |

**Step 3:** Drain spinach and chop. Mix with onion and cheese and spread over bread. Cut the other 4 slices of bread in half and place over spinach.

| | | | | | |
|---|---|---|---|---|---|
| 3 | | **eggs** | 3 | | |
| 1½ | cups | **milk** | 375 | mL | |
| ½ | tsp | **salt** | 2 | mL | |

**Step 4:** Beat together eggs, milk and salt. Pour over all. Let sit for 1 hour in a cool place. Bake for about 40 minutes.

**Variations**

• You can bake this right away but it is better to let it sit for 1 hour before baking.
• Use fresh spinach or swiss cheese.
• Add a little nutmeg to the milk.

*(Source: Basic Shelf Cookbook)*

## What else can I eat with the tofu balls?

white sauce *or* mushroom gravy

pasta *or* rice

carrots *or* beans *or* broccoli

pineapple slices

### Did you know?

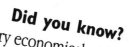

- Tofu is very economical, rich in protein, iron and calcium.
- It is quick to prepare. There is no waste and it keeps for about a week if you store it in water in the fridge.

### Hint

- This is a good way to try tofu if you have not used it before.
- For stir-fry, salads, soups, or chili buy the firm or extra-firm type.

# Tofu balls

**4 servings**
**Cooking time: 15 minutes**

| | | | | | |
|---|---|---|---|---|---|
| ³/₄ | lb | **firm tofu,** mashed | 375 | g | |
| 1 | small | **onion,** finely chopped | 1 | | |
| ½ | cup | **bread crumbs**<br>*or* **quick cooking oats** | 125 | g | |
| 3 | tbsp | **soya sauce** | 50 | mL | |
| 1½ | tbsp | **peanut butter** | 25 | mL | |
| ½ | cup | **parsley** | 125 | mL | |

**Step 1:** Mix all ingredients together. Form into 24 balls.

**Flour**
**Oil**

**Step 2:** Roll balls in flour and fry in oil until brown on all sides. Turn gently.

## Variations

• Leave out the parsley and the balls still taste good.
• You can bake the balls at 425°F (220°C) for 15 minutes.
• Stuff 3 or 4 tofu balls into pita bread with cucumber, tomato and lettuce.

# What else can I eat with the zucchini frittata?

carrot sticks

salad

whole wheat bread

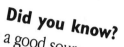

## Did you know?

- Zucchini is a good source of Vitamins A and C.
- Strips of raw zucchini make excellent "dippers."

## Hint

- In place of 1 egg you can use 2 egg whites. This reduces the cholesterol in a meal.

# Zucchini frittata

**2 – 3 servings**
**Cooking time: 10 minutes**

| | | | | | |
|---|---|---|---|---|---|
| 1 | tbsp | **oil** | 15 | mL | |
| 1 | med | **onion,** sliced | 1 | | |
| 2 | | **zucchini,** sliced | 1 | | |
| ¼ | tsp | **pepper** | 1 | mL | |

**Step 1:** In a nonstick frying pan cook vegetables in oil for 5 minutes.

| | | | | | |
|---|---|---|---|---|---|
| 1 | can | **Romano beans,** drained (19 oz / 540 mL) | 1 | | |
| 3 | | **eggs** | 3 | | |
| 1 | tbsp | **Parmesan cheese** | 15 | mL | |

**Step 2:** Stir in beans. Mix eggs and cheese. Pour over beans. Reduce heat to low. Cover and cook for 10 minutes or until egg is set.

## Variations

- Add some sliced mushrooms.
- Add a little chopped green or red pepper and / or tomatoes.
- Add some leftover potato slices.
- Try some other beans, such as pinto or white kidney beans.

# Soups

*H*OME-MADE SOUPS STILL TASTE the best, but keep some canned and dried soups on hand for a quick meal when you are in a hurry. Try different combinations of vegetables, herbs and spices, and experiment once in a while with beans, lentils and split peas. Soup often tastes even better when you warm it up the next day, so cook enough for two meals—and enjoy! ❧

# What else can I eat with Amanda's lentil soup?

whole wheat bun

*or* grilled cheese sandwich

milk

fruit

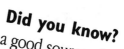

## Did you know?

- Lentils are a good source of iron, fibre and protein.
- Lentils are not only good for you, they are also economical, and they taste good, too.
- Barley is also a good source of fibre.

## Hint

- Green or brown lentils take about 45 minutes to cook. They keep their shape well and are good for soups, casseroles and salads.
- Split red lentils cook in 10–15 minutes and are good for quick soups or in vegetarian spaghetti sauce.

# Amanda's no recipe lentil soup

**6 – 8 servings**
**Cooking time: 1 hour**

| | | | | |
|---|---|---|---|---|
| 1 | cup | **lentils,** green *or* brown | 250 | mL |
| ½ | cup | **barley** | 125 | mL |
| 6 | cups | **water** | 1.5 | L |
| 1 | tbsp | **oil** | 15 | mL |

**Step 1:** Wash and drain lentils. In a large pot, bring water, lentils and barley to boil. Turn down heat and simmer for 30 minutes. Add oil to reduce foaming.

| | | |
|---|---|---|
| 2 | cans | **tomatoes** (19 oz / 540 mL) |
| | | **vegetables** (carrots, onion, celery, cabbage, mushrooms, zucchini) |
| | | **Salt & pepper** |
| | | **Thyme, marjoram** |

**Step 2:** Add tomatoes and your favourite combination of vegetables. Bring to a boil again. Turn down heat and simmer for about 30 minutes or until vegetables are tender.

## Variations

- Be creative with this soup. Use your favorite vegetables in season.
- Add a little grated cheese to each serving bowl.
- Leave out barley and add dumplings instead: Mix 1½ cups (375 mL) flour, 2 tsp (10 mL) baking powder, ½ tsp salt (2 mL), 1 cup (250 mL) milk and 1 egg. Drop dough into hot soup. Cover and cook for 12–15 minutes.

# What else can I eat with the bean and tomato soup?

whole wheat bread

apple sauce

## Did you know?

- You can save time and money if you buy cheese on sale, grate it and freeze it for later use.
- You can also freeze a block of cheese. When it thaws the cheese crumbles, but you can use it for cooking.

## Hint

- A can of soup can be the base for a quick meal.
- Vegetable or minestrone soup—add canned beans of your choice and some cheese.
- Broth—stir a raw egg into the hot soup and add some veggies and egg noodles.

# Bean and tomato soup

**2 – 3 servings**
**Cooking time: 15 minutes**

| | | | | | |
|---|---|---|---|---|---|
| 1 | can | **beans in tomato sauce** (14 oz/398 mL) | 1 | | |
| 1 | can | **tomatoes** (19 oz/540 mL) | 1 | | |
| 1 | small | **onion,** chopped | 1 | | |
| ½ | tsp | **basil** | 2 | mL | |
| ½ | cup | **parsley,** chopped (optional) | 125 | mL | |

**Step 1:** Cut up tomatoes in can. Chop onion. Combine beans, tomatoes, onion and basil in a large pot. Bring to a boil. Simmer for about 15 minutes. Stir occasionally.

| | | | | | |
|---|---|---|---|---|---|
| ½ | cup | **light Cheddar cheese,** grated, shredded or cubed | 125 | mL | |

**Step 2:** Spoon soup into bowls and sprinkle with cheese.

## Variations

- Add a little cooked meat.
- Add frozen or cooked leftover vegetables.
- Add cooked leftover rice or pasta.
- Add a little chili powder.

# What else can I eat with the broccoli soup?

scrambled egg on toast

ice cream and cookie

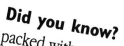

### Did you know?

- Broccoli is packed with nutrients. Here are some: Vitamin C, folate, beta carotene, calcium and iron. It even has some protein and is a high source of fibre.

### Hint

- This soup tastes great warmed up the next day.
- Use broccoli often, cooked or raw, in soups, stir-frys, casseroles or with a dip.

# Broccoli soup

**6 servings**
**Cooking time: 1 hour**

| | | | | | |
|---|---|---|---|---|---|
| 8 | cups | **water** | 2 | L | **Step 1:** In a large pot, bring water and chicken soup base to a boil. |
| 2 | tbsp | **chicken soup base** | 25 | mL | |

**Step 1:** In a large pot, bring water and chicken soup base to a boil.

| | | | | | |
|---|---|---|---|---|---|
| 1 | med | **onion,** sliced | 1 | | |
| ½ | cup | **celery,** sliced | 125 | mL | |
| 1 | | **potato,** cubed | 1 | | |
| 1 | lb | **broccoli** | 500 | g | |

**Step 2:** Slice onion and celery. Peel potato and cut into cubes. Cut up broccoli. Add vegetables to boiling water. Bring back to boil and simmer for 30 minutes.

| | | | | | |
|---|---|---|---|---|---|
| 2 | tbsp | **cornstarch** *or* **flour** | 25 | mL | |
| 1 | cup | **milk** | 250 | mL | |

**Step 3:** In a cup mix together cornstarch and milk. Add to soup. Bring to boil again and cook until thickened.

## Variations
- Add a handful of shredded cabbage to the vegetables.
- Add a few cubes of ham or grated light Cheddar cheese.
- Use canned evaporated milk to make the soup creamier.
- Quick broccoli soup: Cook some broccoli, add a can of mushroom soup, some milk and a little grated cheese.

# What else can I eat with the hamburger soup?

whole wheat bun *or* garlic toast
*or* Loretta's bannock (p. 116)
fruit yogurt

## Did you know?
• Beans and vegetables take longer to get soft if you add tomatoes at the beginning of cooking.

## Hint
• Cook enough soup for 2 meals.
• Freeze leftover vegetables and use in soups and stews.

# Hamburger soup

**6 – 8 servings**
**Cooking time: 1 hour**

| | | | | | | |
|---|---|---|---|---|---|---|
| 1 | lb | **hamburger** | 0.5 | kg | **Step 1:** In a large pot, cook onion and hamburger until meat starts to brown. Drain off fat. |
| 1 | cup | **onion,** chopped | 250 | mL | |
| 1 | cup | **potatoes,** cubed | 250 | mL | **Step 2:** Prepare vegetables and add to meat. |
| 1 | cup | **carrots,** sliced | 250 | mL | |
| 1 | cup | **cabbage,** shredded | 250 | mL | |
| ¼ | cup | **rice,** uncooked | 75 | mL | **Step 3:** Sprinkle rice over meat and vegetables. |
| 6 | cups | **water** | 1.5 | L | **Step 4:** Add water and seasonings. Cover and simmer for about one hour. |
| ½ | tsp | **thyme** | 2 | mL | |
| 1 | tbsp | **salt** | 15 | mL | |
| | | **Pepper** | | | |
| 1 | can | **tomatoes** (14 oz / 398 mL) | 1 | | **Step 5:** Add tomatoes. Heat and serve. |

**Variations**

- Use leftover or frozen vegetables.
- Use barley instead of rice.

# What else can I eat with the quick potato soup?

whole wheat bun and coleslaw (p. 103)

*or* spinach salad (p. 105)

*or* tomato sandwich

milk

cookie

## Did you know?

- Potatoes are a good source of Vitamin C, especially in the fall. It is best to store potatoes loose in a cupboard. Do not store potatoes in the fridge or in a plastic bag.

## Hint

- You can make an even faster soup if you have leftover mashed potatoes. Just add some milk and onion. Mix and heat.

# Quick potato soup

**3 – 4 servings**
**Cooking time: 20 minutes**

| | | | | | |
|---|---|---|---|---|---|
| 4 | large | **potatoes,** cut up | 4 | | |
| 2 | med | **carrots,** sliced | 2 | | |
| 3 | cups | **water** | 750 | mL | |
| 1 | small | **onion,** chopped | 1 | | |

**Step 1:** Prepare vegetables. Combine water and vegetables in a large pot and bring to a boil. Reduce heat and cook in covered saucepan for 15 minutes. Do not drain. Mash vegetables.

| | | | | | |
|---|---|---|---|---|---|
| 2 | cups | **milk** | 500 | mL | |
| 1 | tsp | **salt** | 5 | mL | |
| | | **Pepper** | | | |

**Step 2:** Add milk and seasonings. Heat but do not boil.

## Variations

- Use a can of evaporated milk in place of regular milk.
- Add grated cheese.
- Add cooked, sliced wieners.
- Add a can of mushroom soup.
- Add some parsley or some marjoram.

# What else can I eat with Susan's cabbage soup?

grilled cheese sandwich

muffin *or*

rice pudding

## Did you know?
- Nutritionists believe that cabbage, broccoli, cauliflower and brussels sprouts contain substances that may help to reduce the risk of certain cancers.

## Hint
- Eat cabbage more often.
- Cabbage is nutritious and cheap, and it keeps well. It can be used in many different ways, e.g., in coleslaw, in soup, stir-fried, creamed, in cabbage rolls or baked in layers with ground beef and tomato soup on top.

# Susan's cabbage soup

**5 – 6 servings**
**Cooking time: 1 hour**

| | | | | | |
|---|---|---|---|---|---|
| 8 | cups | **water** | 2 | L | **Step 1:** In a large pot, bring water and soup base to boil. |
| 2 | tbsp | **chicken soup base** | 25 | mL | |
| 1 | can | **crushed tomatoes** (14 oz / 398 mL) | 1 | | **Step 2:** Slice onion and carrot thinly. Shred cabbage. Add vegetables and tomatoes to boiling water. Bring back to boil and simmer for about one hour. |
| 1 | med. | **onion** | 1 | | |
| 1 | large | **carrot** | 1 | | |
| 4 | cups | **cabbage** | 1 | L | |

**Variation**

• Quick cream of cabbage soup: Cook 10 cups of shredded cabbage and 1 sliced onion in 2 cups chicken stock. Make a white sauce from $\frac{1}{3}$ (75 mL) cup oil or margarine, $\frac{1}{3}$ cup (75 mL) flour and 2 cups (500 mL) milk. Add to cabbage. Season with salt and caraway seeds.

# Salads

**S**ALADS ADD COLOUR, TEXTURE AND variety to our meals. You do not need a lot of fancy or expensive ingredients to make a salad. Try some new combinations of ingredients for a side salad. Or add some cheese cubes, boiled eggs, chickpeas, tuna or salmon to create a light meal — and enjoy! 🐦

## Recipes in this section

# What else can I eat with the anything goes macaroni salad?

cucumber and tomato slices
hot dogs
buns
fruit in yogurt

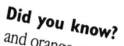

### Did you know?

- Dark green and orange vegetables and orange fruit (e.g., broccoli, carrots, cantaloupe) are high in Vitamin A. Include some every day.

### Hint

- This salad makes a great summer meal by itself. It is also a tasty side dish for a barbecue.
- Use leftover pasta for this salad.
- To make a potato or kidney bean salad, simply use cooked potatoes or kidney beans instead of macaroni.

# Anything goes macaroni salad

**4 – 6 servings**

| | | | | | |
|---|---|---|---|---|---|
| 2 | cups | **macaroni** | 500 | mL | **Step 1:** Cook macaroni in lots of boiling water until tender. Drain, rinse and cool. |

| | | | | | |
|---|---|---|---|---|---|
| 2 | | **eggs,** hard cooked, chopped *or* sliced | 2 | | **Step 2:** Boil eggs, cool and chop. Add all ingredients to macaroni. Mix together carefully. |
| 1 | cup | **celery,** diced | 250 | mL | |
| 4 | | **green onions,** chopped | 4 | | |
| ½ | cup | **salad dressing** | 125 | mL | |
| | | **Salt & pepper** | | | |

## Variations

- Add grated carrots and green pepper.
- Add ham and cheese cubes.
- Add tuna and peas or beans.
- Add some mustard to the dressing.
- Cook frozen mixed vegetables with the macaroni.
- Cook a package of macaroni and cheese and make into salad.
- Add fresh vegetables such as tomatoes, cucumber, lettuce.

# What else can I eat with the coleslaw?

ham sandwich *or* omelette
macaroni and cheese
*or* meatballs and potatoes

### Did you know?

- Cabbage salads cost very little and can provide a lot of variety and nutrition.
- Cabbage is a good source of Vitamin C.

### Hint

- Try this easy cabbage salad. Toss together:

| | | | |
|---|---|---|---|
| 2 | cups | (500 mL) | shredded cabbage |
| 1 | | | chopped apple |
| ½ | | | chopped orange |
| ¼ | cup | (50 mL) | raisins |
| ¼ | cup | (50 mL) | nuts, optional |
| 1 | tbsp | (15 mL) | oil |
| 1 | tbsp | (15 mL) | lemon juice |

# Coleslaw

**6 – 8 servings**

| | | | | |
|---|---|---|---|---|
| 4 | cups | **cabbage,** shredded finely | 1 L | **Step 1:** Mix together. |
| ½ | cup | **salad dressing** *or* **light mayonnaise** | 125 mL | |

## Variations

- Add ½ cup (125 mL) crushed pineapple.
- Add 1 cup (250 mL) grated carrot.
- Add 1 cup (250 mL) chopped apple.
- Add to the salad dressing:
  3 tbsp (50 mL) milk
  1 tsp (5 mL) sugar
  ½ tsp (2 mL) salt
- Add some pickle juice.
- Add celery seed and some finely chopped onion.
- You can also add a can of corn (12 oz/341 mL), drained.
- Add some raisins—some children really like it.
- For a simple dressing, mix creamy salad dressing or light mayonnaise with enough milk or evaporated milk to pour off the spoon.

# *W*hat else can I eat with the leafy salad plus?

onion bun *or* pita bread

*or* sandwich

yogurt

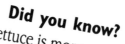

### Did you know?
- Romaine lettuce is more nutritious than iceberg lettuce. The darker the green the more Vitamin A.

### Hint
- There are many low-fat dressings available. Look for the nutrition information on the label. Choose salad dressings with 3 g of fat or less per 1 tbsp (15 mL).
- Make your own dressings. They take very little time to make and cost a lot less than store-bought ones.

# Leafy salad plus

**1 – 4 servings**

## Caesar salad:
    **Romaine lettuce**

    **tuna** *or* **flaked turkey** *or*
    **imitation crab** *or* **cold meat**

    **croutons**

## Spinach salad:
    **spinach**

    **onion slices** *or* **mushrooms** *or*
    **boiled egg** *or* **bacon** *or* **cheese**

    **orange slices**

**Step 1:** Combine your favorite ingredients with a dressing of your choice.

## Variation

• Try this creamy dressing instead of a bought one. It will keep for about a week in the fridge.

| 1 | cup | (250 mL) | yogurt |
| ½ | cup | (125 mL) | light mayonnaise |
| 1 | tbsp | (15 mL) | lemon juice |
| ⅓ | cup | (75 mL) | chopped parsley |
| | | | dill, garlic, mustard, salt and pepper to taste |

# What else can I eat with the white kidney bean salad?

whole wheat crackers *or* bread

carrot sticks

milk

## Did you know?

- Some people like white kidney beans better than red kidney beans because the skins are softer.
- It is cheaper to cook beans from scratch than to buy them canned. Try pinto beans or black-eyed peas for a change.

## Hint

- How to cook beans:
Bring 2 cups (500 mL) beans and 6 cups (1.5 L) water to a boil. Turn off heat and let stand for one hour. Drain and rinse beans. Add 6 cups of water again and cook till tender (1–1½ hours). Drain. This makes about 5 cups.

# White kidney bean salad

**2 – 3 servings**

| | | | | | |
|---|---|---|---|---|---|
| 1 | can | **white kidney beans,** drained (19 oz/540 mL) | 1 | | |
| ⅓ | cup | **onion,** finely chopped | 75 | mL | |
| ½ | cup | **celery**, finely chopped | 125 | mL | |
| 1 | | **apple,** diced | 1 | | |
| ½ | tsp | **salt** | 2 | mL | |
| 2 | tbsp | **mayonnaise** | 25 | mL | |

**Step 1:** Combine all ingredients in a large bowl and serve.

## Variations

• Add a few cubes of low fat cheese.

• Add ½ tsp (2 mL) bacon bits.

• You can use red kidney beans or pinto beans instead of white kidney beans.

# Sweet Treats

**ANY PEOPLE LIKE CAKES,** cookies and desserts but may feel guilty about eating them. In a healthy diet there is room for a variety of foods. Plan your meals and snacks, and use foods higher in fat or calories only once in a while. Choose sweet treats that include fruits, whole grains and lower fat dairy products more often—and enjoy! ❧

## Apple bread pudding

4 – 6 servings
350°/180°C
Baking time: 1 hour

| | | | | | |
|---|---|---|---|---|---|
| | | | | | **Step 1:** Turn oven on. Grease 2 qt (2 L) baking dish. |

**Step 1:** Turn oven on. Grease 2 qt (2 L) baking dish.

| 6 | | **slices bread**, white or brown | 6 | |
|---|---|---|---|---|
| 2 | | **apples** | 2 | |

**Step 2:** Cut bread and apples into small pieces. Place half the apples in baking dish. Add bread, apples again and finish with bread.

| 4 | | **eggs** | 4 | |
|---|---|---|---|---|
| 2 | cups | **milk** | 500 | mL |
| 2 | tbsp | **oil** | 25 | mL |
| 1 | tsp | **cinnamon** | 5 | mL |
| ⅓ | cup | **sugar (white or brown)** | 75 | mL |

**Step 3:** Mix eggs, milk, oil, cinnamon, and sugar in a bowl. Pour egg mixture over bread and apples.
Bake for about one hour or until the pudding is set in the centre.
Serve warm or cold. Test with a toothpick; it will come out clean when done.

## Variations

- Use ⅔ cup skim milk powder and 2 cups water in place of milk.
- Add raisins to the apple layer.

## Banana loaf

**1 loaf**
**350°F/180°C**
**Baking time: 50 – 60 minutes**

|  |  |  |  |  | **Step 1:** Turn oven on. Grease loaf pan. |
|---|---|---|---|---|---|
| 3 |  | **bananas** | 3 |  | **Step 2:** Mash bananas. |
| ⅓ | cup | **margarine** *or* **shortening** | 75 | mL | **Step 3:** Blend margarine and sugar together. |
| ⅓ | cup | **sugar** | 175 | mL | Beat in eggs. |
| 2 |  | **eggs** | 2 |  | Stir in mashed bananas. |
| 1⅓ | cups | **flour** | 375 | mL | **Step 4:** Mix dry ingredients and add to |
| 2 | tsp | **baking powder** | 10 | mL | banana mix. Stir only until flour just |
| ⅓ | tsp | **salt** | 1 | mL | disappears. Pour batter in loaf pan. Bake for 50 – 60 minutes. Insert toothpick in centre of loaf. If it comes out clean, the banana loaf is done. |

**Variation**
- Add ¼ cup raisins and/or ½ cup mixed candied fruit and/or ½ cup walnuts.

**Hints**
- This loaf freezes well.
- You can freeze mashed bananas or pieces of bananas and use later for baking.

# Bran muffins

**9 large or 12 small**
**400°F / 200°C**
**Baking time: 15 – 20 minutes**

**Step 1:** Turn oven on. Grease muffin tins.

| | | | | |
|---|---|---|---|---|
| 1 | cup | **flour** | 250 | mL |
| 2 | cups | **wheat bran** | 500 | mL |
| 1 | tsp | **baking soda** | 5 | mL |

**Step 2:** In a large bowl mix dry ingredients.

| | | | | |
|---|---|---|---|---|
| ½ | cup | **molasses** | 125 | mL |
| 1 | | **egg** | 1 | |
| ¼ | cup | **oil** | 50 | mL |
| 1 | cup | **milk** | 250 | mL |

**Step 3:** Stir together liquid ingredients in another bowl. Add to flour mixture. Stir just enough to moisten. Do not over mix. Fill muffin tins or paper baking cups. Bake for 15 – 20 minutes.

## Variations

• Add ½ cup (125 mL) dried raisins, nuts or chocolate chips.
• Use quick oats instead of bran.
• Or try this: 1 cup (250 mL) flour, 1 cup (250 mL) wheat bran, ¼ cup (50 mL) sugar, 1 tbsp (15 mL) baking powder, 1 egg, 1 cup (250 mL) milk and 2 tbsp (25 mL) oil. Follow Steps 1 to 3.

# Fruit crisp

**4 – 6 servings**
**350°F/180°C**
**Baking time: 30 – 35 minutes**

**Step 1:** Turn oven on.
Grease 2 qt (2 L) baking dish.

| | | | | | |
|---|---|---|---|---|---|
| 3 | cups | **fruit,** sliced | 750 | mL | |
| 1 | tbsp | **sugar** | 15 | mL | |

**Step 2:** Spread fruit in baking dish.
Sprinkle with sugar.

| | | | | | |
|---|---|---|---|---|---|
| ½ | cup | **oats,** quick cooking | 125 | mL | |
| ½ | cup | **brown sugar** | 125 | mL | |
| ¼ | cup | **flour** | 50 | mL | |
| ¼ | cup | **margarine** | 50 | mL | |

**Step 3:** In a bowl combine oats, brown sugar and flour. Cut in margarine till mixture is crumbly. Sprinkle over fruit. Bake for 30 – 35 minutes.

## Variation
• Use your favorite fruit—apples, peaches, rhubarb, strawberries, blueberries—fresh, canned or frozen.

## Hints
• Sprinkle a little lemon juice on the apple so it will not turn brown.
• Put regular oats in blender and use instead of quick cooking oats.

# Rose's bannock (bread)

450°F / 230°C
Baking time: 12 – 15 minutes

**Step 1:** Turn oven on.

| | | | | |
|---|---|---|---|---|
| 6 | cups | **flour** | 1.5 | L |
| ½ | tsp | **salt** | 2 | mL |
| 3 | tbsp | **baking powder** | 50 | mL |
| ½ | cup | **margarine** | 125 | mL |

**Step 2:** Mix dry ingredients in one bowl. Cut in margarine

| | | | | |
|---|---|---|---|---|
| 2 | cups | **water** | 625 | mL |
| ½ | cup | **milk** | 125 | mL |

**Step 3:** Make a well in the centre of the flour mixture. Pour water and milk into well. Starting at the centre gradually mix flour into liquid until a soft dough forms. Knead in the remaining flour very gently.

**Step 4:** Place dough on ungreased cookie sheet. Flatten dough and prick with a fork. Bake until golden, about 12 – 15 minutes. Serve warm with soup or stew or eat with butter and jam. Warm up leftover bannock in the microwave.

**Variation**

• Add 1 cup (250 mL) grated cheese or ½ cup/125 mL raisins to dough.

# Never fail chocolate cake

**350°F / 180°C**
**Baking time: 30 minutes**

**Step 1:** Turn oven on.
Grease 8" (2 L) baking pan.

| | | | | |
|---|---|---|---|---|
| 1½ | cups | **flour** | 375 | mL |
| 3 | tbsp | **cocoa** | 50 | mL |
| 1 | tsp | **baking soda** | 5 | mL |
| 1 | cup | **sugar** | 250 | mL |
| ½ | tsp | **salt** | 2 | mL |

**Step 2:** Mix ingredients together.

| | | | | |
|---|---|---|---|---|
| ⅓ | cup | **oil** | 75 | mL |
| 1 | tbsp | **vinegar**, white | 15 | mL |
| 1 | tsp | **vanilla** | 5 | mL |
| 1 | cup | **cold water** | 250 | mL |

**Step 3:** Add to dry ingredients.
Pour into pan.
Bake for 30 minutes.

## Hints

- You can buy cocoa in the bulk food section.
- Make your own hot chocolate mix:

| | | | | |
|---|---|---|---|---|
| 4 | cups | **skim milk powder** | 1 | L |
| ¾ | cup | **cocoa** | 175 | mL |
| 1 | cup | **sugar** | 250 | mL |

Combine ½ cup mix with 1 cup boiling water.

# Vanilla creams

| | | | | | |
|---|---|---|---|---|---|
| ⅓ | cup | **margarine** | 75 | mL | |
| ⅓ | cup | **flour** | 75 | mL | |
| 2 | cups | **milk** | 500 | mL | |

**Step 1:** In medium saucepan melt margarine. Stir in flour. Cook for a minute. Add milk. Beat with wire whisk to prevent lumps. Cook and stir until thickened.

| | | | | | |
|---|---|---|---|---|---|
| 2 | | **eggs** | 2 | | |
| 2 | tbsp | **sugar** | 25 | mL | |
| 1 | tsp | **vanilla** | 5 | mL | |

**Step 2:** Beat eggs, sugar and vanilla together. Add to sauce and cook for another 5 minutes. Pour into a bowl or individual dishes. Cool.
Serve with some banana slices and brown sugar or with some jam or sprinkle with coconut.

**Hint**

• To keep brown sugar soft, store in an airtight container and add a piece of apple or bread to the sugar.

**SIMPLE MEALS FOR SMALL BUDGETS**

# ORDER FORM

*Available for only $9.95\* each (plus GST)*

**Purchase Instant Chef 2 at any GMCC Bookstore:**

- City Centre Campus: 10700 – 104 Avenue; call 497-5482
- Mill Woods Campus: 7319 – 29 Avenue; call 497-4082
- Jasper Place: 10045 – 156 Street; call 497-4383

**OR**
Mail the order form below.

✂ - - - - - - - - - - - - - - - - - - - - - - - - - - - - - - - - - - - - - - - - - - - -

Name: _____

Address:_____

_____

P.C.: _____ Phone: _____

Mail completed order form and payment by cheque, money order, or Visa/Mastercard to:

**Bookstore,
Grant MacEwan Community College,
Mill Woods Campus
7319 – 29 Avenue
Edmonton, AB, T6K 2P1
Email: bookstore@gmcc.ab.ca**

**Grant MacEwan
Community College**

**PLEASE SEND ME _____ COPIES OF INSTANT CHEF 2**

____ *(# of copies)*  x  $_____ *(price)*  =  $ _____

**Plus GST**  7% x  Quantity  = $ _____
**Plus HST**  15%  (Maritimes Only) = $ _____
**Plus Shipping & Handling**
(Add $2.50 for 1 – 10 copies; add $5.00 for 10 or more)  $ _____

| **TOTAL ENCLOSED =** | $ _____ |

Visa/Mastercard # _____ Exp. Date _____

Receipt Required _____ yes _____ no

**\*Discounted price of $7.95** +GST available on orders of 10 or more.

Office Mail Date: _____